ROTHERHAM PUBLIC LIBRARIES

Witness History Series

WAR IN THE TRENCHES

Stewart Ross

Wayland

Titles in this series

The Arab-Israeli Conflict
Blitzkrieg!
Britain between the Wars
Britain since 1945
China since 1945
The Cold War
The Home Front
The Industrial Revolution
The Origins of the First World War
The Russian Revolution
South Africa since 1948
The Third Reich
Towards European Unity
The United Nations
The USA since 1945
War in the Trenches

Cover illustration: 'Three men and a machine gun can stop a battalion of heroes.' Defensive weapons assumed particular importance during the First World War. Armed with machine guns, small groups of soldiers were able to defend their positions against vastly superior numbers.

First published in 1990 by
Wayland (Publishers) Ltd
61 Western Road, Hove
East Sussex BN3 1JD, England

Editor: Alison Cooper
Designer: Nick Cannan
Consultant: Terry Charman, historian and researcher
  at the Imperial War Museum

British Library Cataloguing in Publication Data
Ross, Stewart
  War in the trenches. – (Witness history series: ISSN
00955–761X)
  1. World war. 1. Western front.
  I. Title II. Series
  940.4144

  ISBN 0–7502–0007–3

Typeset by R. Gibbs & N. Taylor, Wayland
Printed by G. Canale & C.S.p.A., Turin
Bound in France by A.G.M.

Contents

Over by Christmas?

THE WORLD WAR that broke out in the late summer of 1914 was primarily a European conflict. On one side stood the forces of the Triple Entente: Russia, France and Britain, the latter two supported by soldiers and supplies from their extensive overseas empires. Several smaller countries, in particular Belgium and Serbia, were allied to the Entente, and it was further strengthened when it was joined by Italy (1915) and the USA (1917). Ranged against the Entente were the German and Austro-Hungarian armies of the Dual Alliance, aided in the east by the Ottoman Empire.

The fighting began when the Austro-Hungarians declared war on Russia's ally, Serbia, on 28 July 1914. This was the final stage in a struggle for control of the Balkans which had lasted for years. The countries of Europe had been busily locking themselves into a system of alliances since the late nineteenth century. Now that two countries from opposing camps were at war, it was almost inevitable that their allies would be drawn into the conflict. And so it turned out. With the exception of Italy, by 4 August all the major countries of Europe were at war.

Both sides were confident that the fighting would be short-lived. The future British prime minister, Harold Macmillan, wrote:

> *The general view was that it would be over by Christmas. Our major anxiety was by hook or by crook not to miss it.* [1]

Allies and enemies: the nations of Europe during the First World War.

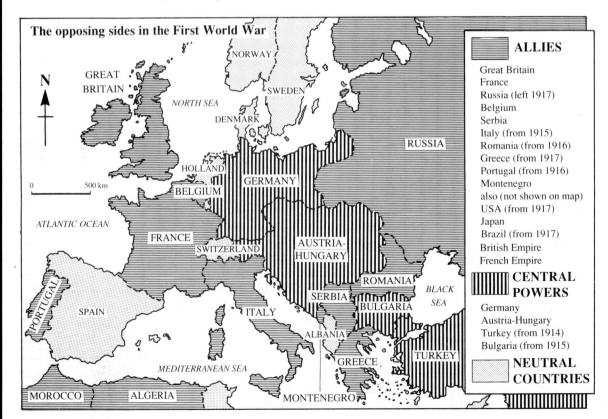

The opposing sides in the First World War

ALLIES
Great Britain
France
Russia (left 1917)
Belgium
Serbia
Italy (from 1915)
Romania (from 1916)
Greece (from 1917)
Portugal (from 1916)
Montenegro
also (not shown on map)
USA (from 1917)
Japan
Brazil (from 1917)
British Empire
French Empire

CENTRAL POWERS
Germany
Austria-Hungary
Turkey (from 1914)
Bulgaria (from 1915)

NEUTRAL COUNTRIES

British confidence was based on the belief that the Royal Navy would drive all enemy ships from the seas, then blockade Germany and force it to surrender. It was thought that in the meantime the 'steamroller' armies of the Russian Empire and the huge French forces, supported by the British Expeditionary Force, would be more than a match for the battalions of the Central Powers. On the other hand, the well-armed and highly-trained German armies believed that they could take the French by surprise with their Schlieffen Plan, encircle Paris, and so end the war within a matter of months. As it turned out, both sides were horribly mistaken. By Christmas 1914 the war had hardly begun.

▼ The outbreak of war was greeted with patriotic demonstrations all over Europe. German students rejoiced at the news but few were still smiling by Christmas.

WAR DECLARED.

NOTE REJECTED BY GERMANY.

BRITISH AMBASSADOR TO LEAVE BERLIN.

RIVAL NAVIES IN THE NORTH SEA.

BRITISH ARMY MOBILIZING.

GOVERNMENT CONTROL OF RAILWAYS.

The following statement was issued from the Foreign Office at 12.15 this morning:—

Owing to the summary re-

AWAITING THE DECLARATION.

THE SCENE AT THE FOREIGN OFFICE.

PATRIOTIC DEMONSTRATIONS.

A large crowd gathered at the entrance to Downing-street last evening to await the first news of the German reply to the British ultimatum. As the evening wore on, the crowd became denser, and excitement grew. The German reply was not expected before 11 p.m. Towards 11, a number of visitors and members of the permanent staff of the Foreign Office gathered in the corridors, which were brilliantly lighted. But the expected dispatch from Sir Edward Goschen was unaccountably delayed. For reasons which can only be surmised, the German Government appears to have delayed it.

Information from a reliable quarter nevertheless reached his Majesty's Ministers, shortly before 11, that the British demand for assurances in regard to the neutrality of Belgium had been summarily rejected. The necessary decisions were therefore taken, and an official statement was issued to the effect that, in consequence of this rejection, his Majesty's Ambassador at Berlin had received his passports and that his Majesty's Government had declared to the German Government that a state of war existed between Great Britain and Germany as from 11 p.m.

Notwithstanding the lateness of the hour, several members of the Diplomatic Corps called

THE KING

SURE SHIELD HER

MESSAGE TO

The following dressed by his Admiral Sir Joh

At this grave history I send t the officers and you have assur ance of my co direction they old glories of t once again the her Empire in th

The above municated to th all stations outs

COMMAND O

The Admiralty night:—

With the appro Admiral Sir John has assumed sup Fleets, with the Rear-Admiral Ch been appointed to Both appointme

▲ *The Times* announces that Britain is at war with Germany.

1

THEATRES OF WAR
The Western Front

TRENCH WARFARE is most closely associated with the Western Front. From the winter of 1914 to the summer of 1918 the front ran due south from the Belgian coast to the River Somme east of Amiens. It then curved east along the River Aisne to Verdun, before snaking south-east to the Swiss border.

The war in the west began with the German invasion of Luxemburg on 1 August. The French and Germans, recalling the way they had fought each other in 1870–1, were prepared for a war of movement, not stagnation. Few commanders appreciated the lessons of the American Civil War (1861–5) and the Russo-Japanese War (1904–5), when soldiers had dug trenches to protect themselves against the fire power of modern weaponry.

It was several weeks before defensive tactics came to dominate on the Western Front. The principal French defences faced the German frontier provinces of Alsace and Lorraine; the German Army bypassed them by invading from the north-west, through

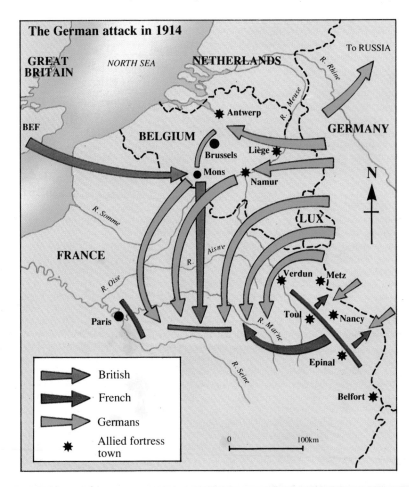

The German attack on Paris in the autumn of 1914. The original plan, abandoned in 1914, was to encircle the French capital from the west.

French soldiers huddle miserably in the trenches in December 1914. Later, trenches were lined with wooden boards to make them more habitable during the winter.

neutral Belgium (2 August). This was the first phase of Germany's Schlieffen Plan. The aim was to defeat France before its ally, Russia, could mobilize, so that the German Army could avoid having to fight a war on two fronts. The Plan failed when, moving east of Paris, the Germans were halted at the Battle of the Marne (5–10 September) and forced to retreat. Both sides now 'dug in', ordering their men to construct trenches in which they could shelter from deadly artillery bombardments and machine-gun fire. By November 1914 the line of the Western Front had been established.

The rest of the war was spent trying to break this deadlock. In 1915 the Germans attacked at Ypres, the French at Champagne and Vimy Ridge, and the British at Neuve Chapelle, Festubert and Loos. Although half a million men were lost, neither side achieved a breakthrough. The next year saw a determined German attack at Verdun (defended by General Pétain, whose watchword was '*Ils ne passeront pas*' – 'They shall not pass'), and a costly British offensive on the River Somme. In 1917 Allied attacks along the River Aisne and at Vimy Ridge, Ypres and Cambrai were repulsed.

The stalemate broke only in 1918. Fresh American troops had reinforced the Allies. In March, the Germans launched what became known as the Ludendorff offensive. When this failed, the Allies, now under the supreme command of General Foch, broke through the enemy lines and forced them to retreat. But when an armistice was signed on 11 November 1918, the Germans were still fighting on French and Belgian soil.

A clash of empires

The Russian armies met the forces of Germany and Austria-Hungary along the Eastern Front. The speed of the Russian mobilization surprised the Central Powers, but the Germans counter-attacked in late August and early September 1914. They crushed the Russians at Tannenberg and the Masurian Lakes, inflicting heavy casualties and taking thousands of prisoners. For the Russians, worse was to follow. In 1915 General Hindenburg won another battle at the Masurian Lakes, while further south General Falkenhayn's Gorlice-Tarnow offensive drove them from Galicia and Poland, and captured vast areas of Russia itself.

The last great campaign of the Eastern Front began in June 1916, when the Russian General Brusilov advanced towards the Carpathian Mountains to take the pressure off his allies in the west. But the heavy casualties and the havoc caused to the country's supply and transport systems helped to bring about the revolutions of 1917. The Russian armies disintegrated, and with the Treaty of Brest-Litovsk (March 1918) the Bolshevik government accepted Germany's humiliating terms for peace. Although there was more movement on the Eastern Front than in the west, trenches were widely used, and the slaughter was just as horrifying as in France and Belgium.

Russian prisoners taken at the Battle of Tannenberg. The German victory showed that the Russian forces were not an unstoppable 'steamroller'.

The war spread to many other parts of the globe, including the Far East, Africa and the Middle East. Trench warfare, however, was confined almost exclusively to European campaigns. These took place in south-eastern Europe and northern Italy as well as on the Eastern and Western Fronts. The fighting in the Balkans began with a disastrous Austro-Hungarian assault on Serbia. A year and a half later the heavily outnumbered Serbian Army finally surrendered. Romania succumbed to an attack by combined armies of the Central Powers and withdrew from the war in May 1918. The most extended trench warfare in the Balkans took place from April 1915 to January 1916 on the Gallipoli Peninsula. A large force of Allied troops was pinned down along the coast and had to be

Italian artillery abandoned by the roadside in the retreat from Caporetto. Why do you think that guns captured from the enemy could not always be reused by the victors?

withdrawn after months of inconclusive fighting.

Italy joined the war in 1915 and launched a series of offensives against Austria-Hungary in the foothills of the Alps. For many months neither side made any significant advance, as their armies became bogged down in the type of trench warfare which was already familiar elsewhere. In late 1917, however, the Austro-Hungarians launched the massive Caporetto offensive and drove back the Italians almost to Venice. Little movement followed until the Allies successfully counter-attacked in the summer and autumn of 1918.

2
STALEMATE
'They shall not pass'

SOLDIERS WERE FIRST ordered to dig trenches so that they could have some temporary shelter from enemy gunfire. A trench was a long gash in the earth, a ditch hewed out by hand to a depth of around two metres and wide enough for two men to walk past each other. The soil from the trench was piled up in front to form a parapet, beneath which a firing step was cut so that infantrymen could stand and see over the top towards the enemy. Although a simple idea, the trench was an excellent device for removing men from the line of fire. As long as they kept their heads down, troops in the trench were safe from rifle or machine-gun bullets; only a direct hit by an artillery shell could cause much damage.

Trenches had some major drawbacks. If the enemy managed to reach the parapet, the men inside were sitting targets for rifle fire or

The Western Front, 1914–18. The unbroken line of trenches made it impossible to attack the enemy's flanks and forced the generals to resort to assaults on the front-line defences.

The Western Front, 1914-1918

N

- - - - -	Frontiers 1914
—— · —— ·	Limit of German penetration 1914
——	Line of prolonged trench warfare
• • • • •	Line on 11th November 1918

Consolidating the front line: German troops building a dug-out and a trench early in the winter of 1914. Why do you think it was not normally possible to work in daylight and in the open like this?

bayonet attack. To prevent this happening, trenches were cut in zig-zag formation and protected with rolls of barbed wire. There were usually at least three rows of trenches (in some places the Germans had twelve), connected with zig-zagging communication trenches. Trenches were also vulnerable to attacks from the flank – it was to avoid this that the Western Front stretched from the North Sea to Switzerland.

Another major problem with trenches was that they were not intended to be inhabited for long. They offered little shelter from the weather and when it rained they soon filled with water. Shortly after he had arrived at the front line in France, the writer Robert Graves

remembered hearing a fellow officer talking about his life in the trenches:

> *When I came out here first, all we did in trenches was to paddle about like ducks and use our rifles. We didn't think of them as places to live in . . . Now we work here all the time, not only for safety, but for health. Night and day.*[2]

Why do you think the man to whom Graves spoke felt it necessary to work on the trenches for reasons of health?

However, once a network of trenches had been established, strengthened with machine-gun posts and fronted with barbed wire, it became almost impossible for infantrymen or cavalry to break through. That is why on the Western Front the First World War stagnated into a long-drawn-out and dismal war of attrition.

Guns and mud

A major reason why there was so little movement on many fronts during the First World War was that defensive strategy and weapons were better developed than those of offence. In other words, it was easier to stay put than to advance. In both attack and defence, artillery was seen as the crucial weapon: 'It was a gunners' war'.[3] However, when used to support an advance, artillery could often hinder rather than help an army's forward movement. Why was this?

A favoured tactic was to bombard the opposing lines for several days before an attack was due to start, with the aim of destroying the enemy's front-line defences and wearing down its morale. However, the prolonged artillery bombardment gave the men in the trenches opposite plenty of warning of an attack and thus time to prepare for it. The biggest gains were in fact made when the enemy was taken unawares.

Much of the fighting on the Western Front took place in low-lying areas which in peacetime were drained by miles of canals and ditches. The picture below shows what happened to this sort of terrain when it was subjected to an artillery bombardment. A British soldier described the landscape he had to cross in an advance:

> As far as the eye could see was a mass of black mud with shell holes filled with water. Here and there broken duckboards, partly submerged in the quagmire; here and there a horse's carcass sticking out of the water; here and there a corpse. The only sign of life was a rat or two swimming about . . .[4]

The Ancre valley on the Western Front, 1916. Heavy artillery fire has transformed the landscape into a wasteland of blasted trees, mud and stagnant pools of water.

It is not difficult to imagine why it was hard for infantry to advance over such terrain, and almost impossible for heavy artillery to move forward to support it. Even when infantry managed to overrun the enemy positions, the delay in bringing up the heavy guns meant that the advantage was lost.

There were other reasons why artillery proved incapable of breaking the deadlock. J. M. Bourne, a British historian, suggests two of them:

> *Inaccuracy was a major weakness . . . Artillery was not only inaccurate but also inefficient . . . The greater part of the British artillery consisted of shrapnel-firing field guns . . . [which were] largely ineffective against barbed wire, earthworks and concrete dug-outs.*[5]

August 1917. Even in summer, the mud was sometimes so deep that guns became bogged down.

A British soldier recalls the inaccuracy of his own artillery:

> *Through some blunder our artillery barrage opened up about two hundred yards short of the specified range and thus opened right in the midst of us. It was a truly awful time – our men getting cut to pieces . . . by our own guns.*[6]

Though heavy artillery might have been unreliable as a weapon supporting an advance, the shrapnel-firing field gun was a deadly way of halting an attack, 'responsible more than any other single factor . . . for the costly ineffectiveness of infantry assaults'.[7]

13

The machine gun

The machine gun was a nineteenth-century invention. But even as late as 1914 very few officers on either side realized its true potential. At the start of the war the French had just 2,500 machine guns for the entire Army, and the British allowed for only two for each battalion of about 850 men. The Germans had about the same number of guns, though they were better deployed and therefore more effective. By the end of the war the British had set up a Machine Gun Corps and equipped their Army with one machine gun for every two platoons (60–80 men). Other armies had made similar increases in their provision of the weapon.

Why were machine guns considered so important? The answer was one of plain statistics. The Vickers gun could fire 450 rounds per minute, while in the same time an experienced infantryman could fire only fifteen aimed rounds. This gave the machine gun thirty times the fire power of a rifle. Although machine guns were more expensive than rifles to produce, they were a relatively cheap source of fire power, as Sir Eric Geddes explained to the British Secretary of State for War, Lord Kitchener:

> *I told Kitchener that rifles and machine guns were the same as shillings and pounds: that nine rifles were equal to a Lewis automatic gun and thirteen rifles to a Vickers machine gun . . .*[8]

Machine guns in action near Ypres.

Scenes such as the one described below became all too familiar on the battlefields of the Western Front:

Newly-arrived American soldiers being taught how to handle a Vickers light machine gun. The gun had already acquired a fearsome reputation.

> *The long burst of a machine gun does not kill a battalion; indeed, some men in a line will almost certainly pass through the run of bullets, in the gaps between them, so to speak. But if the line of men perseveres with determined gallantry, over a long open approach, the end is certain. So it was before Y Ravine. The Newfoundland officers and men would not halt; they had orders to advance into the enemy line: they advanced. 710 men fell.*[9]

In a grossly mismanaged attack on the first day of the Battle of the Somme (1 July 1916) the British lost 57,470 men, of whom 19,240 were killed. As one German machine gunner recalled: 'They went down in their hundreds. You didn't have to aim, we just fired into them.'[10] The age of mechanized warfare had arrived. Bravery was no longer enough.

British machine gunners set up their outpost in a cottage – and wait.

15

Barbed wire

Though the words of this song might appear rather sick to us, it was only by making light of their experiences that the soldiers could cope with the conditions they faced.

Barbed wire was invented by Joseph Glidden in 1874 and used first in the USA as a cheap and effective fencing material. It did not take long, however, for soldiers to realize how it could be used in warfare. The British employed it during the Boer War (1899–1902) as a means of combating Boer guerrilla tactics.

The advantages of barbed wire were numerous, since it was:
- Cheap to manufacture.
- Light and easy to transport, especially when produced in rolls.
- Quick to put in position.
- Very difficult to remove, particularly by men under fire.

Artillery bombardment tended just to blow the wire into the air, leaving it largely intact when it fell back. The only certain way to remove a barrier of barbed wire was to cut it. Night patrols were sent out with the task of repairing their own wire or cutting through

A barbed-wire gate used as a block against enemy raiding parties. Of course, it offered no protection from bullets; trenches were cut in zig-zags to prevent raiders from getting a clear line of fire at soldiers defending their positions.

that of the enemy. Such exercises were extremely dangerous, as the soldiers had to creep out across no man's land, right up to the trenches opposite. The writer Siegfried Sassoon recalled how difficult it was to make an impression on a 'hedge' of barbed wire:

> When I started I soon discovered that cutting tangles of barbed wire in the dark in a desperate hurry is a job that needs ingenuity . . . More than once we were driven in by shells . . . Two men were wounded and some others were reluctant to resume work. In the first greying of dawn only three of us were still at it . . . We had been working three and a half hours, but the hedge hadn't suffered much damage.[12]

British troops going 'over the top' through their own barbed wire at the Battle of the Somme, 1916.

Barbed wire proved an extremely effective barrier against both infantry and artillery attack. As one infantry officer remembered:

> Barbed wire terrified and obsessed the infantryman. All his daring and courage came to nought when he ran against an incompletely destroyed network. He knew he would get caught and lacerated in its entangled mass.[13]

The only serious drawback was that soldiers making an attack were sometimes hampered by the protective wire lying in front of their own trenches.

17

Weapons and equipment

It is important to remember that during the First World War (as in any war) what was supposed to happen rarely did. Most of the soldiers on all fronts were amateurs who had volunteered or been conscripted from ordinary civilian jobs. After a basic military training, they were expected to pick up knowledge and skills at the front. Moreover, it was unusual to find a front-line soldier who was fully equipped. The result was frequent confusion and chaos.

The rifle and bayonet were the basic pieces of equipment supplied to soldiers of all armies. The British .303 Lee-Enfield rifle, with a ten-round magazine, was probably the best standard service weapon issued during the war. It was a relatively expensive and complicated gun, however, which needed frequent cleaning to operate effectively. Why do you think that it was not always easy in the trenches to keep dirt out of the moving parts? Dirt was also a problem for machine gunners, armed either with the light Lewis gun or the larger, water-cooled Vickers machine gun.

The latter gun weighed 18 kg and required a heavy tripod and water tank to operate.

Weapons were rarely available in the numbers required. In September 1914 the British were short of rifles and had scarcely any hand grenades. They did not have enough artillery shells until 1917, and only in 1918 were sufficient numbers of guns being produced.[14] Not only was the equipment in short supply, but some items were also poorly designed. For example, by July 1916 steel helmets were widely available for use by British soldiers, but they were too heavy to be worn with comfort.

During an attack an infantryman was expected to carry his rifle, bayonet, grenades and a huge assortment of other equipment including:

- Extra clothing
- A gas mask
- A full water bottle
- 170 rounds of ammunition
- A shovel
- Wire cutters
- Sandbags (unfilled!)
- Toiletries and medical kit
- A portable cooking stove and fuel
- Mess tins
- 'Iron rations', consisting of corned beef, sugar, tea and biscuits

All this equipment weighed over 30 kg! The unfit men who went 'over the top' were expected to carry this burden over no man's land, then have enough strength left to fight the enemy. One infantryman wrote that the grenades in his pocket were so heavy that they made his trousers fall down. When he stopped to pull them up he fell behind his colleagues in the attack. This probably saved his life.[15]

Like the attackers, defenders had to wear heavy kit during a battle. Here German troops are defending a trench against a British attack. Can you identify any of the weapons and equipment shown in the picture?

New recruits being provided with uniforms. They do not seem to be very happy with what is going on.

Early anti-aircraft defences – an American-designed Lewis machine gun mounted on a post.

3
ATTACK
The right tactics?

BEFORE THE DEVELOPMENT of tanks and aircraft, there were only two methods by which an army could attack its enemy. One was the direct frontal assault, charging on foot or on horseback. The other involved outflanking the enemy, in order to attack from the side or the rear. The only way to get round the line of trenches along the Western Front was to concentrate forces elsewhere in Europe, a strategy discussed on page 26. Otherwise, troops had to advance directly towards the enemy in front of them. By 1918 two methods of attack had been tried, one more successful than the other.

A major offensive was made on the River Somme during the summer of 1916. It was preceded by a massive bombardment (audible in London) over eight days along a twenty-nine-kilometre front. A force of half a million men (mainly British but supported by five divisions of French troops) attempted to advance across no man's land. The horror of a frontal assault through muddy conditions is well documented:

> *We fell into the mud and writhed about like wasps crawling from rotten plums . . . The dead and wounded were piled on each other's backs . . . The second wave, coming up from behind, were knocked over in their tracks and lay in heaving mounds . . . Those unable to crawl into the sloping shell holes were doomed.*[16]

German wounded line a railway station platform after the Battle of the Somme in 1916.

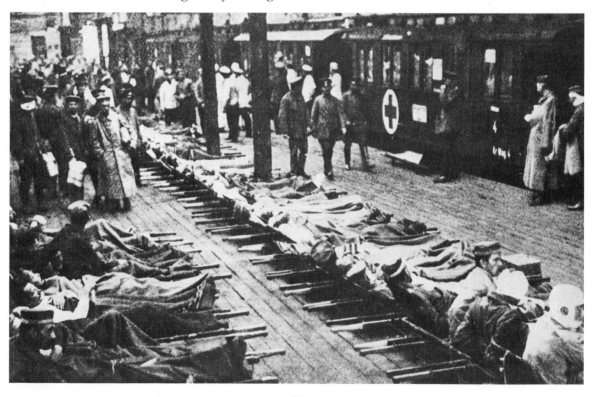

By the end of November, the British had progressed ten miles at the furthest point and lost 419,000 men, most of whom were volunteers. No British army had ever experienced such casualties before and one writer has commented that 'the nation never recovered'.[17] According to the official British history, the Germans lost 650,000 men, though some historians believe the true figure to be lower, at around 450,000.[18] It has been claimed that the Somme was 'the muddy field grave of the German Army'.[19] Can you see why Field Marshal Haig, the British Commander-in-Chief, claimed that the Somme offensive had been a success?

The second type of offensive was used by the German General Ludendorff in March 1918. A key element was surprise. After a short intensive artillery bombardment, the

A British soldier is caught in the glare of an exploding incendiary shell. Star shells and flares, which exploded high over the lines, were also used at night as each side tried to discover what the enemy was doing.

Germans attacked with trench mortars and gas, concentrating on a few weak points in the Allied line. They were more concerned with moving forward than with taking strong points held by the enemy, and their strategy produced considerable territorial gains.

The last offensives of the war were launched by the Allies, whose weary forces had by now been strengthened by troops and materials from the United States. These successful attacks were supported by large numbers of tanks and aircraft. They marked the end of trench fighting and the beginning of a new phase of warfare.

'Gassed last night'

Both sides experimented with new weapons which they hoped might help to break the deadlock on the Western Front. The most unpleasant of these was poison gas. The French used tear-gas grenades in August 1914, but the Germans were the first to employ gas extensively. This gave them the advantage of surprise, but it also provided the Allies with a useful propaganda weapon: they were quick to point out that the use of poison gas confirmed the Germans as a 'barbaric' people, who would stop at nothing to win the war. However, it was not long before the Allies followed their enemy's example.

A German soldier recalled the decision to use gas:

In the middle of January [1915] I received orders to go and see Geheimrat Haber. . .[at] the Ministry of War. He explained to me that the Western Fronts, which were all bogged down, could be got moving again only by means of new weapons. One of the weapons contemplated was poison gas, particularly chlorine, which was to be blown towards the enemy from the most advanced positions.[20]

Machine gunners in gas helmets during the Battle of the Somme.

In this extract from the diary of a British Captain, you can see one of the major problems of using gas against the enemy:

Towards morning the wind . . . seemed to be blowing . . . from the German trenches towards us. However, the order was to let loose the gas, but when those in charge of the cylinders turned on the taps, clouds of gas blew backwards . . . One of the gas men . . . became overcome and was lying at my feet groaning horribly.[21]

Later this problem was overcome by firing gas in shells.

Another development was the use of mustard gas, the advantages of which you can work out from the next extract. A British company had been warned of a gas attack and had put on their masks:

After wearing them for some time . . . [the men] thought the original alarm was false as no gas had been smelt. What they did not know was that this was mustard gas, had no smell, and had delayed action . . . By nightfall every officer and man was either dead or in hospital.[22]

22

▲ Soldiers blinded by tear gas during the Ludendorff offensive in 1918.

▶ A well-protected sentry ringing the alarm to warn of a gas attack.

Poison gas was often used before an attack, to wear down the enemy's morale, and in the course of the war it caused over a million casualties. However, it never proved a decisive weapon. It was unreliable and involved the men on both sides dressing in cumbersome protective masks and clothing. Can you imagine what it was like trying to fight when wearing one of the gas masks shown in the pictures?

Tanks – the secret weapon

The idea of an armoured vehicle with tracks was first suggested in 1914, though the first operational tank did not enter service until early in 1916. Private Charles Cole remembers seeing his first tank:

> *Something was brought near to the reserve trench, camouflaged with a big sheet. We didn't know what it was and were very curious and the Captain . . . said, 'You're wondering what this is. Well, it's a tank,' and he took the covers off and that was the very first tank.*

The name 'tank' is supposed to have been used to confuse the Germans into believing that the vehicle was a water tank. Why do you think so much secrecy surrounded the new weapon?

The mighty tank – breaking through barbed-wire defences, October 1917.

What Private Cole saw next demonstrated the secret weapon's strengths and weaknesses. The first tanks were very unreliable:

> *Well, we were at the parapets . . . and waiting for the tank. We heard the chunk, chunk, chunk, chunk, then silence! The tank never came . . . We couldn't wait for it, we had to go over the top . . . and we got cut to pieces . . .*

But eventually the tank lurched into action:

> *The Germans ran for their lives – couldn't make out what was firing at them . . . they didn't know anything at all about tanks, so the tank went on, knocked brick walls, houses down, did what it was supposed to have done – but too late![23]*

British soldiers set up their headquarters in a Mark I tank knocked out during the Battle of Flers-Courcelette in 1916.

As well as being unreliable, the interiors of early tanks were so noisy and uncomfortable that crews could not operate them for more than a few hours. The Germans had little faith in the new machines, and it was a long time before the British and French were able to use them effectively. Tank after tank was swallowed up by the Flanders mud. In November 1917, the Tank Corps found an area of firmer ground at Cambrai. They attacked *en masse* for the first time, broke through the enemy lines and advanced eight kilometres. However, the infantry could not keep up with the tanks. The Germans brought up their reserves and the advantage was lost.

On 8 August 1918, 600 tanks were launched at the German trenches and, in what became known as the 'black day of the German Army', 324 got through.[24] This time, the initial gains were followed up and the Allies clawed back much of the ground gained by the Germans in the Ludendorff offensive. The tank had come of age.

A German flame-thrower in action against a British tank. The crew had little chance of survival if their vehicle caught fire.

Alternative strategies

Although tanks were eventually to prove the most successful of the new devices used on the Western Front, in June 1917 the British enjoyed a remarkable local victory at Messines, employing an age-old tactic, popular since Roman times. Secretly burrowing below the enemy defences, the Royal Engineers constructed a gigantic mine beneath the German positions along the Messines Ridge. The completed tunnel was then filled with almost half a million kilogrammes of high explosives; when the charge was detonated, a large part of the ridge was destroyed. In the ensuing battle the Germans lost 25,000 men and another 7,000 were taken prisoner. The Allies lost 17,000 men. The success was not followed up quickly enough to lead to a complete breakthrough.

Even more imaginative were the Allied plans to land behind the German lines. Schemes to put men ashore on the Belgian coast and in Schleswig-Holstein never materialized. But further afield attempts were made to break the deadlock by penetrating the Central Powers' southern flank. The wisdom of such a strategy was hotly debated in Britain at the highest levels. By 1915 Winston Churchill, then First Lord of the Admiralty, and Lloyd George, the two principal 'Easterners', were despairing of ever achieving a breakthrough on the Western Front. Supported by Kitchener, the Secretary of State for War, they demanded that landings be made in the eastern Mediterranean. The 'Westerners', professional soldiers commanding the armies in France and Belgium, declared that Germany

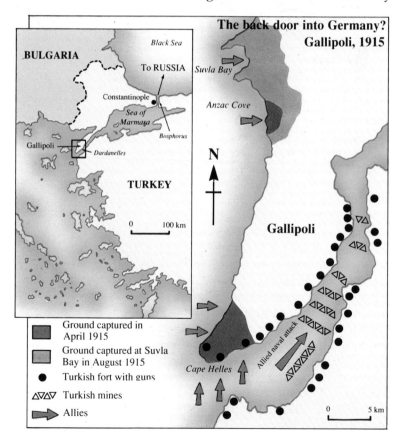

The Gallipoli Peninsula. The aim of the Allied expedition was to force a passage into the Black Sea and relieve the hard-pressed Russian forces.

Allied forces being evacuated from 'W' Beach, Gallipoli on 7 January 1916. Although the expedition was a total failure, the withdrawal was carried out with surprising efficiency.

could never be beaten by such tactics, which would turn out to be mere side-shows.

In the end two landings were made, one at Gallipoli in the Dardanelles (25 April 1915), and another at Salonika (3 October 1915). Both were dismal failures. At Gallipoli, the troops were pinned down on the rocky shoreline and the campaign rapidly deteriorated into trench warfare. The Allied forces – from France, Britain and the colonies, especially Australia and New Zealand – suffered about a quarter of a million casualties before they were withdrawn eight and a half months later. The army at Salonika remained stuck behind massive barbed-wire emplacements for most of the war. Only in Italy were Allied troops able to be of much use in southern Europe. Several divisions were sent there after the disastrous Italian defeat at

Caporetto (October-November 1917), and they helped to make possible the Allied victory at Vittorio-Veneto a year later.

With some justification the 'Easterners' blamed poor organization and leadership for the failure of their strategy. However, the historian A.J.P. Taylor points out the flaw in their plan. What do you think he means when he says that the 'Easterners':

> . . . wanted to turn the German flank, to find . . . a back-door into Germany. [But] the hard fact, not made plain on the maps, was that there was no such back-door except Russia . . . North-eastern Italy, Salonika, the Dardanelles led nowhere, or were, at best, doors firmly bolted by nature in Germany's favour.[25]

4

IN THE TRENCHES
At the front

IN THE EARLY MONTHS of the war, when the battle lines were being established, trenches were little more than ditches, with no adequate provision for sleeping accommodation. As it became clear that there was little prospect of an early end to the fighting, the commanders on all fronts began to pay greater attention to the comfort and safety of the men in the trenches. Can you imagine the importance of this in raising the morale of the troops?

The Germans were acknowledged to be the builders of the best trenches. The lines attacked by the British on the Somme in 1916 were provided with deep concrete bunkers. One British infantryman noticed that a captured German dug-out had been made with imported British cement! Towards the end of the war the Germans constructed an even more formidable array of defences,

known as the Hindenburg Line. This consisted of concrete and steel forts in three lines, covering a depth of several miles. This 'defence in depth' made a complete breakthrough more difficult to achieve.

British trenches were generally much less carefully prepared, though in 1916 the men were provided with shell-proof shelters for the first time. Robert Graves gives two examples of the different types of trench he came across. The first shows how comfortable the officers could make themselves:

> . . . this dug-out happened to be unusually comfortable, with an ornamental lamp, a clean cloth, and polished silver on the table . . .
> Pictures pasted on the papered walls; spring-mattressed beds, a gramophone, easy chairs . . .[26]

British troops occupying a captured German dug-out. The quarters were far more comfortable than most of those found in the Allied lines.

'Well, if you knows of a better 'ole, go to it.' Do you think cartoons that made light of the terrible conditions were good for the soldiers' morale?

The second example gives a graphic illustration of the brutalizing effect of war, in its description of the materials used to build the parapet:

> Among the Cuinchy brick-stacks . . . the trenches
> have made themselves rather than been made,
> and run . . . in and out of the big thirty-foot-high
> stacks of bricks . . . The parapet of a trench which
> we don't occupy is built up with ammunition
> boxes and corpses. Everything here is wet and
> smelly.[27]

Not all trenches were just squalid burrows. Many were lined with wood or corrugated iron, to support the earth walls and make the trenches more comfortable. But this was still the enduring memory of most infantrymen:

> Nothing to see but bare mud walls; nowhere to
> sit but on a wet muddy ledge; no shelter of any
> kind against the weather except the clothes you
> are wearing; no exercise you can take in order to
> warm yourself.[28]

Health and sickness

Most governments made sure that the men in the trenches did not go hungry, even though there were shortages of food at home. Why do you think they did this? The troops received plenty of tinned food, bread, jam and biscuits and the British also produced food called Maconochie, 'a meal in a tin', which was quite popular. Nevertheless, the rations were dull and sometimes inedible.

Soldiers in the front lines were rarely provided with fresh food and they frequently suffered from acute constipation. Drinking water was often in short supply, as it had to be carried to the lines in cans. The chemicals which were added to purify it left a horrible taste, though British troops always had plenty of tea which helped to make a more palatable drink. Much alcohol was consumed in the trenches. Some men found that only by drinking could they cope with the horrors around them. British officers drank whisky; other ranks were almost always given a tot of rum to boost their courage before an attack.

Men soon became infested with lice, and louse hunting became an inevitable part of the daily routine. Soldiers spoke of using matches to roast them out of clothing and of the satisfactory crunch as the insects were crushed between the fingernails. Rats were also a problem and there was the constant worry that they would spread disease.

Soldiers of the East Yorkshire Regiment having their feet inspected by a medical officer in the winter of 1918. Trench foot was caused by wearing wet boots for days on end and it crippled thousands of front-line infantrymen.

Sickness was as great a problem as enemy gunfire. Troops exposed to damp, cold weather soon fell victim to bronchitis and pneumonia. Trench lavatories were disgusting, and dysentery and similar complaints were common. In the summer of 1915, it was estimated that more than three-quarters of the Allied troops at Gallipoli were suffering from some form of intestinal illness.[29] Troops who were obliged to wear wet boots for long periods of time often suffered from the particularly unpleasant disease of trench foot. The victim's feet began to rot, and often they had to be amputated.

An officer inspecting a trench, 1915. In some areas, trenches were wet and muddy for most ot the year. Working in such conditions, it is hardly surprising that so many troops became ill.

There was a daily medical parade, when a doctor or medical orderly checked up on the complaints common to trench life, such as swollen feet, stomach upsets, lice, boils, and flu. The terrible mental strain of life at the front, known as 'shell-shock', was not properly understood at first. Some of the 346 British soldiers shot for cowardice were really suffering from mental exhaustion or depression.[30]

Stretchers!

In 1914, the British Royal Army Medical Corps (RAMC) had 1,000 doctors, supported by 500 female nurses from Queen Alexandra's Royal Army Nursing Corps (known as the QAs). When trench warfare began they were totally overwhelmed by the number of casualties they had to handle. By the time of the armistice the strength of the RAMC had been considerably increased and there were 50,000 QAs to assist them. But they still could not cope with the thousands of wounded who flooded back from the lines after a major offensive.

The handling of casualties was organized in five stages. The responsibility for bringing men in from the battlefield lay with the Regimental Stretcher Bearers, many of whom were conscientious objectors. These brave and respected men had the daunting task of collecting the wounded from no man's land and the trenches, and taking them back to the Regimental Aid Post. The work of the stretcher bearers and at the Aid Post was often performed under fire and in terrible conditions: in the winter it could take up to six men to carry a stretcher through the mud. It was not uncommon for wounded soldiers to lie unattended in no man's land for days.

After receiving first aid at the Aid Post, the wounded walked, or were carried, to a field dressing station, still within range of enemy fire. Here a medical officer decided on appropriate treatment for the casualties. Surgery was carried out at field hospitals, known as casualty clearing stations, several kilometres behind the lines. One doctor has described the heart-breaking nature of his work:

> [After an attack] We surgeons were hard at it in . . . a hut holding four tables. Occasionally we made a brief look around to select from the thousands of patients those few we had time to save. It was terrible.[31]

German prisoners help to move wounded men to a field hospital by light railway.

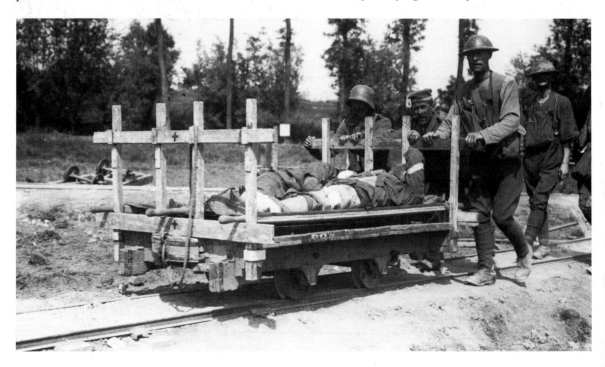

A field dressing station, 1916. Dressing stations were set up close to the front line, often in shell-damaged buildings and surrounded by debris.

Casualties declared 'beyond surgical aid' were left to die. The others were given what help was available, then transferred to a hospital on the French coast or in Britain. The wounded had to make use of whatever transport was available: the lucky ones travelled by ambulance; others had to make do with barges, lorries or even converted cattle trucks.

Thousands of men died in hospitals and dressing stations because medical science was not sufficiently advanced to cope with their wounds. There were no antibiotics; blood transfusions were rare before 1917; gas gangrene infected exposed flesh; and the horrible mutilation caused by shrapnel presented doctors with situations for which they had virtually no training. One writer described the army medical services as 'tragically inadequate'.[32]

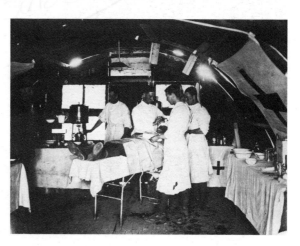

Australian doctors operate on a wounded soldier in a dressing station.

Routine

Strange though it may seem, one of the problems of trench life was boredom. Although the enemy might be as little as fifty metres away across no man's land and there was always danger from mortar or shell-fire, large-scale attacks were rare. For much of the time soldiers were cooped up in narrow trenches, often cold and wet, without exercise or much variation in the daily routine. The poet Wilfred Owen wrote about this aspect of trench life:

The poignant misery of dawn begins to grow . . .
We only know war lasts, rain soaks and clouds
sag stormy.
Dawn massing in the east her melancholy army
Attacks once more in ranks on shivering ranks of
grey,

But nothing happens.[33]

At night most men tried to sleep, although the periodic gunfire prevented them from sleeping for more than three or four hours. Others stood on sentry duty, peering out over the dark waste of no man's land. (In daylight they often used periscopes so that they could see over the parapet without presenting a target.) Listening posts were established to warn of German tunnelling under the Allied positions. The correct procedure if mining activities were suspected was to sink a bucket of water into a hole and look for ripples caused by vibrations from enemy tunnelling. One soldier described how, having no bucket, he used a biscuit tin: '[I] soon found that it leaked and I was kneeling in water, the [tin] nearly empty.'[34]

The soldiers filled bags with earth to give their dug-outs more protection from shell-fire.

A break from the fighting: American troops playing cards with their British allies.

Some groups made up wiring parties which ventured out to cut the enemy's barbed wire, or repair their own defences. Night patrols also tried to bring in the wounded who had fallen in no man's land, or made surprise attacks on enemy positions. Occasionally the scene was lit up with brilliant flares. When this happened men froze – if they moved they became obvious targets for snipers.

Dawn was the most dangerous time, when attacks were usually launched. After this came the order 'Stand down', when the soldiers could relax and have breakfast. They then got on with the tasks of the day, such as repairing or improving the trench, bringing up supplies and cleaning weapons. Much of their time was spent sitting chatting, reading or writing letters home. These were heavily censored, in case they fell into enemy hands and gave away vital information about troop

French Canadian soldiers taking a rest from cleaning up their trench.

positions, planned attacks or morale. Many soldiers smoked heavily, which made them unfit. At night it was extremely dangerous to light a cigarette in the open, for a flaring match often attracted a bullet.

5
REACTIONS
Fraternization

ONE OF THE MOST extraordinary events of the whole war took place at Christmas 1914. It is best told in the words of one of the soldiers in a letter home:

> You will hardly credit what I am going to tell you: but . . . Listen.
>
> Last night as I sat in my little dug-out . . ., my chum came bursting in . . . with: 'Bob! Hark at 'em!' And I listened. From the German trenches came the sound of music and singing . . .
>
> I got up to investigate. Climbing the parapet, I saw a sight which I shall remember to my dying day. Right along the whole of the line were hung paper lanterns . . . many of them . . . upon Christmas trees.

Then, after much carol singing and cheerful shouting:

> . . . a party of our men got out of the trenches and invited the Germans to meet them halfway and talk. And there in the searchlight they stood, Englishman and German, chatting and smoking cigarettes together midway between the lines.[35]

Along wide stretches of the line the fraternization continued on Christmas Day and Boxing Day. In some places there were football matches between men who, only a

British and German troops fraternizing in no man's land during the Christmas truce.

What war? A remarkable view of the trenches on the Western Front on Christmas Day, 1914.

few hours before, had been trying to kill each other. Gifts were exchanged and photographs taken. Brief friendships were made. Never had the futility of war been more pointedly demonstrated. The French soldiers, however, took no part in the unofficial Christmas truce. Why do you think they were less willing than their British allies to fraternize with the opposing armies?

The High Commands on both sides were understandably worried by the incident. At Christmas 1915 there were numerous orders forbidding any similar breach of discipline, although in one or two places there was singing and the occasional giving of presents. There were no Christmas truces after that. But, as one officer noted,

> These incidents . . . suggest that . . . educated men have no desire to kill one another; and . . . were it not for aggressive national policies . . . war between civilized peoples would seldom take place.[36]

The Christmas truces indicate that, unlike in the Second World War, there were no clear ideological differences between the two warring sides.

What enemy? German and British wounded walk back from the lines together.

Survival

Robert Graves heard this story of a company attack:

> *The officer . . . signalled them to lie down and open covering fire. The din was tremendous. He saw the platoon on his left flopping down too, so he whistled the advance again. Nobody seemed to hear. He jumped up from his shell hole, waved, and signalled 'Forward!'*
>
> *Nobody stirred.*
>
> *He shouted: 'You bloody cowards, are you leaving me to go on alone?'*
>
> *His platoon-sergeant, groaning with a broken shoulder, gasped: 'Not cowards, sir. Willing enough. But they're all ******* dead.'* [37]

A single machine-gun burst had killed the whole platoon.

The casualty figures for the First World War make dismal reading: [38]

Country	Mobilized Forces	Military Deaths
Austria-Hungary	7,800,000	1,200,000
British Empire	9,496,170	947,023
France	8,410,000	1,385,300
Germany	11,000,000	1,808,545
Italy	5,615,000	462,391
Russia	12,000,000	1,700,000
Ottoman Empire	2,850,000	325,000
USA	4,355,000	115,660

A front-line soldier had little chance of coming through the war unscathed. Junior officers, who were supposed to lead their men

Over the Top, **an evocative painting by John Nash, of British troops struggling into action in 1917.**

in attack and were therefore exposed to the greatest danger, could expect to survive for only a few weeks. The old hands prayed for a 'cushy one' or a 'Blighty one', meaning a wound that would necessitate their being sent home. It was observed that: 'They look forward to a battle because that gives them more chances of a cushy one in the legs or arms . . . In trench warfare the proportion of head wounds is much greater.'[39] Graves remembered one experienced soldier 'laughing through our lines' because he had lost three fingers by deliberately waving his hand above the parapet of his trench. He was shot in the head by a German sniper on the way back to the dressing station. Soldiers made themselves armoured vests, while others lied or cheated to get transferred from the front lines. What do you think was meant by the officer at the front who observed that 'most infantrymen don't believe in the war anymore'? [40]

Some historians see the Battle of the Somme in 1916 as marking a turning point in the mood of the troops. Many of the soldiers who died in that battle were volunteers who had flocked to answer Kitchener's call to arms in 1914. A.J.P. Taylor has written that: 'Idealism perished on the Somme. The enthusiastic volunteers were enthusiastic no longer . . . After the Somme men decided that the war would go on forever.'[41]

▲ 'Old soldiers never say die, they'll simply block the way.' Fighting talk in this cartoon by Bruce Bairnsfather, but after the disaster on the Somme many old soldiers felt that the war would never end.

ROLL OF HONOUR.

107 CASUALTIES TO OFFICERS.

The Secretary of the Admiralty announces the following casualties :—

KILLED, JUNE 30.
Phipps, Mr. Thomas G., Skipper, R.N.R.

INJURED, JULY 2.
Hughes, Flight Sub-Lieutenant Alfred M., R.N.

Reported by the War Office under various dates :—

KILLED.
Anderson, Lieut. D. S., Canadian Infantry.
Baden, Sec. Lieut. R., Bedfordshire Regiment.
Ball, Lieut. J. J. B., Royal Field Artillery.
Buchanan, Capt., F. P., Canadian Infantry.
Davis, Sec. Lieut. O. M., East Yorkshire Regiment.
Hasler, Sec. Lieut. G. H., Bedfordshire Regiment.
Hawdon, Lieut. C., Yorkshire Regiment.
Hodgson, Sec. Lieut. R., Leinster Regiment.
Moseley, Sec. Lieut. H. J. R., Rifle Brigade.
Standrett, Sec. Lieut. W. F., Royal Sussex Regiment.
Whill, Sec. Lieut. C. V., Royal Warwickshire Regiment.
    Previously reported Missing, now reported Killed.
Ford, Lieut. R. B., Canadian Engineers.

Jowett, Sec. Lieut. W. H., Liverpool Regiment.
Popple, Sec. Lieut. G. M., Northumberland Fusiliers.
Wickham, Sec. Lieut. C. F. O., Northumberland Fusiliers.

DIED.
Matthysens, Capt. F. A., Welsh Regiment.

WOUNDED.

Border R.—Edgar, 1940 Cpl. J. G.; Haughin, 2124 Cpl. R.; Russix R.—Standen, 2234 S. H.; Upton, 433 G.; Warriner, 6201 Sgt. A.
Dorset R.—House, 12277 F. G.
Welsh R.—Maloney, 11625 J.
Black Watch.—Campbell, 2017 Cpl. P.; Kerwin, 2777 M.
Northampton R.—Rugby, 17052 A.
R. Berks R.—Gale, 3960 Dmr. E. A.
R. W. Kent R.—Cheeseman, 9616 H.
Yorks L.I.—Pinkerton, 20165 S.; Scholes, 3632 G.
Shrops L.I.—Bickell, 14714 H.; Weeks, 11293 J.
K.R.R.C.—Lawton, 15859 W.
N. Staffs R.—Oates, 9935 H.; Cornwell, 5215 W.; Dunnicliff, 9918 G.; Egerton, 7655 L.-Cpl. S.; Jones, 11144 J.; Peake, 10030 E. T.; Richards, 17224 W. H.; Westman, 8242 T.; Witherow, 8173 W.
Durham L.I.—Fowler, 1924 W.
Highland L.I.—Stewart, 19672 Cpl. P.
Seaforth Highrs.—Cormack, 2782 L.; Park, 4595 J.
R. Irish Rifles.—McManus, 8174 F.
R. Munster Fus.—Flanagan, 8943 D.
Rifle Brig.—Gardiner, 9082 T. S.
London R.—Bradbury, 2942 C. R.; Morant, 2978 L. H.
Hertford R.—Morgan, 2401 L.
    Previously reptd. Wounded, now reptd. Died of Wounds.
R. Fus.—Wilson, 4442 H. H. L.
R. Sussex R.—Veness, 632 G.
K.R.R.C.—Paley, 15934 T.
Wilts R.—Hillier, 18015 E. W.
London R.—Stanton, 2517 J. T.

ACCIDENTALLY KILLED.
Rifle Brig.—Rogers, 4009 Sgt. A. J.
A.S.C.—Newick, M.2/118997 T.

DIED.
Hussars.—Gale, 15222 Sh. Smith H.
R.F.A.—Griffiths, 751 Gnr. W.; Poyner, 15825 Gnr. G. W.
R.G.A.—Pitt, 31209 A.; Verman, 86 Gnr. W.
R.E.—Brett, 12242 Spr. W. H.; Dempster, 64563 Spr. H.; Hart, 67032 Spr. J.; Parmenter, 22818 Spr. R. T.; Rowlands, 51858 Spr. R. S.; Routt, 123784 Pnr. S.; Watts, 42035 L/C. W. J.; Williams, 110028 Pnr. J.; Woolger, 12527 Spr. H.
Grenadier Gds.—Hodges, 13228 L.-Cpl. A.
R. Scots.—Finnigan, 3283 J.
R. Fus.—Gage, 12488 E. C.; Gembling, 16589 A. A.; Heal, 8685 Cpl. A. R.
Devon R.—Kingdom, 3598 Cpl. W. H.; May, 1823 J.; Reynolds, 1688 G.; Smerdon, 3864 L.-Cpl. G.
Somerset L.I.—Brooks, 14753 C. G.
S. Wales Borderers.—Cording, 26858 C.
S. Lancs R.—Green, 10848 H.; Jones, 16391 E.
L. N. Lancs R.—Johnson, 2760 T.
Manchester R.—Nicholson, 2341 W.
Highland L.I.—Vallance, 3033 W.

◀ An extract from the casualty list published daily by *The Times*.

'I don't want to die'

As we have seen, the First World War was not fought between two distinct ideologies such as democracy and fascism. Propaganda tried to convince people that the enemy was uncivilized, and that defeat would lead to untold hardship. But the soldiers at the front knew that the men in the trenches opposite were really not very different from themselves. The British referred to the Germans, almost affectionately, as 'Fritz' or 'Jerry'. Though there were atrocities on both sides, the prevalent attitude among most of the soldiers was summed up in the British song which concluded, 'Oh my, I don't want to die, I want to go home'.[42] In other words, soldiers on both sides were more concerned with getting through the war alive than with defeating the enemy. That is why they welcomed a 'cushy' wound.

The ability of an army to continue fighting in appalling conditions depended on its morale, or spirit. By 1917 Russian troops had lost all confidence in the Tsar and his officers. Whole regiments deserted. Many soldiers joined revolutionary movements and Russia eventually withdrew from the war.

The French Army also experienced serious troubles in 1917. General Nivelle's major offensive on the Aisne failed to achieve the desired breakthrough and the French Army suffered heavy losses. Many troops, demoralized and exhausted, mutinied. British troops remembered French battalions bleating as they were marched forward, indicating that they felt like lambs being

For many of the troops on both sides, the war was simply a matter of obeying orders and trying to survive.

Over-zealous Tommy (far in advance of his objective). "ORL RIGHT. DON'T GET NASTY. I MUST 'AVE COME A BIT TOO FAR. WE'RE NOT EXPECTED HERE TILL NEXT WEEK. SEE YOU LATER. SO LONG!"

taken to slaughter. In the end, though, despite its dreadful casualties, the French Army survived. The British Army held 49,000 courts martial for crimes ranging from drunkenness to desertion. Of the 3,000 men sentenced to death, 346 were shot.[43]

Morale held an army together. It is a complex sentiment, made up of some or all of the factors listed below. Some would have been more important to an individual soldier than others.

- Belief in the cause for which one is fighting.
- Plentiful supplies of food, drink, clothing and weapons.
- Regular rest periods and leave.

American soldiers examining a German dug-out that they have just captured. The arrival of American troops in France boosted Allied morale.

- Comradeship and unwillingness to let one's friends down.
- Pride in one's unit.
- The excitement of battle (perhaps).
- Faith in one's superior officers.
- Patriotism.
- Discipline.
- Careful training.

Why do you think that a modern historian has written that many people find it 'simply inexplicable' that the morale of most troops on the Western Front remained so high?[44]

Blighty

'Blighty', from the Hindustani word for Europe or England, was widely used by British soldiers during the war to refer to Britain. It is important to remember that troops did not spend all their time at the front. Many days were also spent behind the lines, either resting, training or taking local leave. But home leave was the prize most highly desired.

Leave (along with everything else) was organized rather haphazardly in the British Army before 1916. Men could serve for almost a year without a trip home, unless they returned wounded. By the end of the war, however, most soldiers were able to get back to Blighty about every six months, although they were never told when their leave was due. This was done to prevent them shirking responsibilities just beforehand, and to prevent hopes being raised unnecessarily: leave could be cancelled at short notice if an attack was planned.

In Britain the war was talked of as being necessary, and even glorious or magnificent. But men from the front knew differently, and many were unwilling to talk about the war. Can you imagine why a soldier may have found a trip home a disturbing and painful experience? One soldier, who had changed into civilian clothes while on leave, remembers refusing to answer a woman who approached him in the street and asked, 'Why are you not in uniform? Afraid to fight?'[45]

During their few short days of home leave men did their best to relax and forget about the war. Some spent their time dancing and drinking. Others went to light-hearted shows, such as *Chu Chin Chow* or passed their days quietly with their families, dreading the day when they would have to put on their uniform again and travel back to the front.

Many soldiers were unable to get the war out of their minds. While recuperating in hospital in London, Siegfried Sassoon was troubled by horrible nightmares:

> *Shapes of mutilated soldiers came crawling across the floor . . . littered with fragments of mangled flesh . . . A young English private in battle equipment pulled himself painfully towards me . . . there was a hole in his jaw and the blood spread across his white face like ink spilt on blotting paper . . .* [46]

The war had a way of following men, even when they were at home on leave.

Boy scouts helping to look after the wounded at a British hospital.

▲ In London's Trafalgar Square, far from the front line, a woman urges men to join the forces.

◀ And she actually asked me if I didn't think I might be doing something! Me! And I haven't missed a charity matinee for the last three months.' A Punch cartoon criticizing women who refused to help in the war effort.

6

WHO WAS TO BLAME?
The generals

BROADLY SPEAKING, there are three reasons for the shattering impact that the First World War had upon those who lived through it.

1 The scale of the losses was far greater than in any previous war.

2 The major continental armies employed conscription before 1914, and Britain introduced it in 1916. With conscripts making up the bulk of all armies (and therefore of all casualties), virtually every family in Europe suffered loss.

3 After the war people began to ask whether the high casualties had really been necessary. They looked for someone to blame: a scapegoat for Europe's 'lost generation'.

The most obvious targets were the generals. It was claimed that inappropriate tactics were the reason why so many troops had been killed. British criticism focused largely on three commanders: Field Marshal Sir Douglas Haig (Commander-in-Chief 1915–18), his friend and partner General Sir William Robertson (Chief of the Imperial General Staff 1915–18) and Field Marshal Sir John French (Commander of the British Expeditionary Force 1914–15). French now has few defenders – during the Battle of Artois-Loos in 1915, for example, he isolated himself from his field commanders and continued the conflict far longer than was necessary. He was replaced by Haig in December 1915.

The cases against Robertson and Haig are much less clear cut. Both were ambitious and wished to go down in history as the men who had won the war – but the same dream was held by Prime Minister Lloyd George, who

had bitter personal quarrels with them, and by French generals such as Nivelle. In their memoirs and histories the 'Easterners' – those who favoured opening a new front in south-eastern Europe – criticized the commanders for opposing their plans. In simple terms, there are two sides to the argument about Haig, who has been described as 'the most controversial and hated soldier in British history'.[47] Which do you find more convincing?

1 Critics say that he was callous, stubborn and unimaginative, with no regard for men's lives. His 'war of attrition' (in which the enemy would eventually be defeated by

---

"THE DAY GOES WELL."

DETAILS OF THE FIGHTING.

SEMI-OFFICIAL REPORTS.

BRITISH HEADQUARTERS, July 1.

9.30 A.M.—British Offensive. At about half-past 7 o'clock this morning a vigorous attack was launched by the British Army. The front extends over about 20 miles north of the Somme. The assault was preceded by a terrific bombardment lasting about an hour and a half.

It is too early as yet to give anything but the barest particulars, as the fighting is developing in intensity, but the British troops have already occupied the German front line.

Many prisoners have already fallen into our hands, and as far as can be ascertained our casualties have not been heavy.

Censored reporting: The Times's coverage of the first day of the Battle of the Somme. Despite the optimistic report from British HQ, the British Army suffered its heaviest-ever casualties.

being worn down by endless attacks) was largely responsible for the heavy losses on the Western Front. He resisted plans to open up new fronts elsewhere in Europe.

2 Haig's defenders point out that in very difficult circumstances he created a huge first-class army from raw recruits. He was more willing than some of his colleagues to use the new techniques of aerial, chemical and tank warfare. His unflinching confidence and determination sustained the Army through terrible times. Millions would have died whatever tactics had been used and Haig's subordinates never lost faith in him.

▶ **Field Marshal Sir Douglas Haig. Was he an incompetent leader, or a great one? The opinions of historians are divided.**

▼ **A Punch cartoon of February 1917, three months after the Somme offensive came to an end. What do you think the artist is saying about the generals' knowledge of life at the front?**

Major-General (addressing the men before practising an attack behind the lines). "I want you to understand that there is a difference between a rehearsal and the real thing. There are three essential differences: First, the absence of the enemy. Now (*turning to the Regimental Sergeant-Major*) what is the second difference?"
Sergeant-Major. "The absence of the General, Sir."

The politicians

The other obvious group who could be blamed for the way the war had been handled were the politicians. Were they not largely responsible for the outbreak of the war? Did they not appoint most of the commanders? And could they not have negotiated a cease-fire at any stage?

The most obvious example of citizens blaming their political leaders was in Russia, where popular support for the Bolshevik Revolution in 1917 was partly because of heavy losses in the war. After 1918 the German Kaiser Wilhelm II was also criticized in some circles, and there were those in the Allied countries who demanded that he should be hanged as a war criminal. In the

end, however, it became clear that he was really only a figurehead; the direction of the war had been largely in the hands of General Ludendorff and Field Marshal von Hindenburg.

By 1914 the elected government in the British House of Commons was ultimately in charge of the nation's affairs, including the management of the war. In theory at least, the politicians were responsible for what went on in the trenches. At the end of 1916 Prime Minister Asquith was removed because he did not appear to be conducting the war energetically enough. His place at the head of the coalition government was taken by David Lloyd George, who brought new vigour to the

(Marshal Foch to Messrs. Clemenceau, Wilson and Lloyd George) 'If you're going up that road, gentlemen, look out for booby traps.' In 1918, there was a feeling in some circles that the military commanders were reluctant to bring the war to a close.

Haig and Joffre (centre) making a point to David Lloyd George, then Minister of Munitions. Lloyd George rarely found himself in agreement with the generals.

administration. He regarded the way the war was being carried out at the front as 'a dismal narrative of military ineptitude'.[48]

But at that time the relationship between the military and the politicians was not clear cut. Haig had an advantage over the politicians, in that he enjoyed the support of the king, George V. Strategy was the responsibility of the Imperial General Staff; sometimes, it suited the commanders to keep the Cabinet in the dark about the true situation in France. Lloyd George was continually at odds with the Chief of the Imperial General Staff, Field Marshal Sir William Robertson, a strong supporter of Haig's war of attrition. In 1918, he succeeded in having Robertson replaced. However,

Lloyd George was concerned that wrangling between himself and the commanders at the front could have a disastrous effect on morale, particularly as Haig was popular with the ordinary soldiers.

It must also be remembered that the war continued to enjoy popular support in many countries. People who advocated a compromise peace, with neither side claiming victory, had their meetings broken up and newspapers which expressed such views were burnt. The general feeling was that the war must go on until total victory had been achieved. As Taylor has written, 'It was necessary to rouse public opinion to fight the war; and this opinion then made it essential to keep the war going.'[49]

Patriotism and propaganda

If it does not seem fair to blame individuals for the slaughter of the trenches, we still need to explain why it happened. The high casualties were the result of the tactics used and deadly mechanized warfare. But why did men continue to obey orders and fight, when they knew that they were almost certain to be killed or wounded? The most important explanation lies in a mixture of patriotism and propaganda.

Patriotism is the love of one's country. The historian J.M. Bourne has written that the British:

> . . . volunteered because they felt that they were needed and that without them the nation's sovereignty . . . possibly even its very existence would be overwhelmed by 'German militarism'. This belief was very important. It gave the war meaning.[50]

Bourne goes on to point out that soldiers' ideas of their country varied greatly, so it may be better to speak of 'patriotisms'.[51] Dockers' battalions, for example, fought for something very different from public schools' battalions.

Professional soldiers were taken by surprise at the remarkable success of Kitchener's drive to raise a volunteer army. Kitchener himself expected to raise an army of about 100,000 men in the first month of the recruitment campaign; he got half a million. People continued to volunteer in huge numbers and conscription was not introduced until 1916. The poet Rupert Brooke reflected the mood of his generation

Edith Cavell, a British nurse, was shot in 1915 for helping Allied soldiers to escape from German-occupied Belgium. This British propaganda poster makes the most of the incident; what do you think its effect would be on public opinion in Britain and the USA?

MISS EDITH CAVELL MURDERED October 12th 1915

REMEMBER!

"YOUR COUNTRY NEEDS YOU"

Lord Kitchener's famous appeal for men to join the armed forces. The response was so strong that, unlike other countries, Britain did not need to introduce conscription until 1916.

in 1914: 'If I should die, think only this of me/ That there's some corner of a foreign field/ That is forever England.'[52] It was this kind of loyalty that made the slaughter possible.

Governments were not slow to exploit the patriotism of their people, as the famous British recruiting poster above illustrates. False stories were spread about the valour and fairness of one's own troops, and the cruelty of the enemy. When the Germans shot the British nurse Edith Cavell for helping Allied soldiers to escape, they handed the Allies a splendid propaganda weapon.

Propaganda was also directed at neutral countries, in the hope of persuading them to

enter the war on the 'right' side. When the Allies were trying to persuade the USA to enter the war, they announced that the war was being fought to bring 'self-determination' to the subject peoples of the Austro-Hungarian and Ottoman Empires.

The British were perhaps the first to realize the important part which propaganda could play in boosting morale. By 1918, two newspaper tycoons had been employed to help in the campaign. Lord Beaverbrook became Minister of Information and Lord Northcliffe Director of Propaganda to hostile countries. The war was being fought with words, films and pictures as well as bullets.

Lest we forget

THE WAR IN THE TRENCHES had countless repercussions. By the time the fighting stopped, new weapons and tactics had evolved, which meant that trench warfare would never again be used on the same scale. Tanks, aircraft and mobile units dominated future land fighting – in the Second World War, the German tactic of blitzkrieg ('lightning war') grew directly out of the stalemate of 1914–18.

Many people felt that Germany and its allies should be punished for what had happened. The French premier, Clemenceau, was a strong supporter of this view. Why do you think this was? Yet the harsh terms imposed on Germany by the Treaty of Versailles in 1919 led indirectly to the rise of the Nazi Party and ultimately to the outbreak of another European war in 1939.

In January 1918, the idealistic US president, Woodrow Wilson, had put forward his Fourteen Points, proposals which he believed would help to prevent future wars. These led to the formation of the League of Nations, which, during the 1920s, enjoyed some success in settling international disputes. However, the League suffered a major setback when the US Congress refused to support Wilson and voted not to join. The member nations who had survived the war were prepared to go to almost any lengths to avoid another conflict. The politicians of the

Allied leaders meeting at Versailles in France to decide the terms of the 1919 peace treaty. Although not consulted, the Germans had to accept the harsh terms of the Treaty of Versailles; its former allies later received similar punishment.

West adopted a policy of appeasement when confronted with the expansionist policies of Hitler and Mussolini during the 1930s.

The social effects of the war were highly complex. With millions of men called up, women had taken over many of their jobs at home. In Britain, this earned women new political, economic and social freedoms, which were not all lost when peace came. The experience of fighting in the trenches had brought men of all classes together. There was widespread disillusion with leaders from the traditional ruling classes who had led them into the conflict.

Stark war memorials went up all over Europe. Armistice Day (11 November) became a day of international mourning.

French troops in the trenches on the summit of Mount Renand. The First World War left terrible scars on the French landscape and bitter images lived on in people's minds long after the fighting had finished.

The scarlet poppies that grew among the trenches of Flanders have become symbols of the millions who have lost their lives in war. After the last shot had been fired, there were many who wished to forget. For those 'bright young things' who could afford it, the following decade became known as the 'Roaring Twenties', an age of reckless pleasure-seeking, jazz, dancing and fast cars. But the haunting reality of what had happened in those four terrible years could never totally be erased.

Leading figures

Alexei Brusilov (1853–1926), Russian General

The most successful Russian General of the First World War, Brusilov first made a name for himself when commanding the Eighth Army in Galicia. He played an important part in halting the German advance of 1915, and in the following year he was put in command of the whole front. In order to help his hard-pressed Italian allies, in the summer of 1916 he abandoned the war of attrition and launched a massive surprise offensive along a 480-kilometre front. Though the Austro-Hungarians gave way and were saved only by German reinforcements, the effort exhausted the Russian Army. Brusilov later fought for both the Provisional Government and the Bolshevik Red Army.

Winston Churchill (1874–1965), British politician and soldier

Churchill was First Lord of the Admiralty from 1911 to 1915. He was primarily responsible for the Navy's excellent state of preparedness in 1914. Together with Lloyd George, he rapidly became disillusioned with the fighting on the Western Front and strongly advocated the opening of a second front in the eastern Mediterranean. However, when the Gallipoli expedition ended in disaster he lost his post at the Admiralty. He commanded the 6th Royal Fusiliers at the front from November 1915 to May 1916. By the end of the war he had been restored to political favour, serving as a competent Minister of Munitions from June 1917 onwards.

Georges Clemenceau (1841–1929), French statesman

For the first three years of the war Clemenceau ('The Tiger') waged a fierce campaign against what he saw as half-hearted and weak conduct of the war by successive French governments. When he finally became premier in November 1917, Clemenceau organized a strong centralized government dedicated to winning the war at all costs. He worked closely with the military commanders and in April 1918 insisted that Foch be accepted as the Supreme Allied Commander. Clemenceau played a major part in enabling the French to withstand the Ludendorff offensive in the spring of 1918. He demanded an unconditional surrender by the Germans, and insisted on harsh terms being imposed upon the Central Powers at the Paris Peace Conference, which drew up the terms of the Treaty of Versailles.

Ferdinand Foch (1851–1929), French Marshal

Foch was the outstanding French commander of the First World War. He did not believe in a war of attrition but in attack whenever possible. His skills were first seen in the defeat of Germany's Schlieffen Plan in the autumn of 1914. His reputation suffered during the costly and unsuccessful offensives of 1915 and 1916, but in 1918 he was put in overall command of the French and British forces. He used this position to oversee the final Allied offensives.

Douglas Haig (1861–1928), British Field Marshal

Haig was one of the most controversial commanders of the war (see page 44). He led the British Expeditionary Force from December 1915 to 1918, having made a name for himself at the First Battle of Ypres in October–November 1914. Over the next three years he was responsible for the costly strategy of attrition, seeking at the Somme, Arras and the Third Battle of Ypres (known by many people as Passchendaele) to wear down the German armies on the Western Front. His tactics were to some extent justified when his troops won nine remarkable victories over the Germans in the summer and autumn of 1918.

Marshal Hindenburg, the German Commander-in-Chief from 1916 to 1918 and President of Germany, 1925–34, with Ludendorff (left) and fellow German commanders.

Paul von Hindenburg (1847–1934), German Field Marshal

Though he had retired from active service in 1911, Hindenburg was recalled in 1914 to take command of the Eastern Front. Working closely with Ludendorff, who was probably a more competent soldier, Hindenburg's armies defeated the Russians at Tannenberg and the Masurian Lakes, then drove them back further in 1915. In 1916 he replaced General Falkenhayn as German Commander-in-Chief, with Ludendorff as his second-in-command. Until the spring of 1918 he followed a defensive strategy in the west, while advancing in the east, until the Russians accepted the Treaty of Brest-Litovsk. Hindenburg remained in command of his country's forces until July 1919.

The Allied war leaders during a break from discussions at the Versailles conference: (left to right) David Lloyd George of Britain, Vittorio Orlando of Italy, Georges Clemenceau of France and Woodrow Wilson of the USA.

Herbert Kitchener (1850–1916), British Field Marshal

Kitchener was made Secretary of State for War in August 1914 – the first serving officer to hold this position. Realizing that the war would not be over quickly, he played an important part in steadying the British forces in the face of the German advance in the autumn of 1914, then set about recruiting and training a massive new volunteer army for service in the trenches. His poster with the slogan 'Your Country Needs You' is still remembered today. His reputation was undermined by the shortage of shells in 1915, when he was responsible for supply, and by his support for the ill-fated Gallipoli landings. He was drowned on the way to Russia when H.M.S. *Hampshire* sank after hitting a mine.

David Lloyd George (1863–1945), British politician

Lloyd George was a radical Liberal politician, who became Minister of Munitions in 1915 and played a vital part in reorganizing British industry to meet the needs of war on a massive scale. He made little secret of his dissatisfaction with Prime Minister Asquith's rather relaxed style of leadership, and replaced him at the head of the coalition War Cabinet in December 1916. Lloyd George brought new vigour to the war effort; although he quarrelled bitterly with the commanders advocating attrition, he steered the country to victory in 1918.

Erich Ludendorff (1865–1937), German General

Before the war Ludendorff was already well known as an intelligent and vigorous soldier. When hostilities broke out, he served with distinction in the west before moving to the Eastern Front, where he formed a formidable

Marshal Pétain, whose motto at Verdun – 'They shall not pass' – inspired heroic resistance by the French soldiers under his command.

partnership with Hindenburg. As the war progressed, Ludendorff became closely involved in politics, earning himself the reputation of being the 'silent dictator' of Germany from 1916 to 1918. However, the failure of the spring offensive in 1918 was a bitter blow to his confidence, and as the Allies counter-attacked he appeared to lose his nerve. He resigned in October and fled in disguise to Sweden.

Henri Philippe Pétain (1856–1951), French Marshal

In the spring of 1916 Pétain was given the unenviable task of commanding the French garrison at Verdun, which was being subjected to massive German attacks. He reorganized the forces under his control and raised the troops' morale, enabling them to withstand the onslaught. After the failure of General Nivelle's offensive in 1917 he became Commander-in-Chief. With a mixture of tact and firmness he suppressed the mutiny in the ranks of the French army, moulding it into a force capable of resisting the Ludendorff offensive and taking part in the Allied advance towards the German frontier.

Siegfried Sassoon (1886–1967), British soldier and writer

Sassoon was typical of a generation of articulate and talented young men on both sides who, after service in the trenches, became bitterly disillusioned with the war. Sassoon volunteered for the army in 1914, fought with exemplary bravery, was wounded and won the Military Cross. When he started to criticize the conduct of the war, the authorities decreed that he was suffering from 'shell-shock'. He was one of many writers whose war poems helped to create the mood of post-war pacifism.

Important dates

Date	Events
1914	*28 July* Austria-Hungary declares war on Serbia.

1914   *28 July* Austria-Hungary declares war on Serbia.
2 August Germany invades Luxemburg.
3 August Germany invades Belgium.
4 August Britain declares war.
9 August Troops of the British Expeditionary Force arrive in France.
17 August Russia invades East Prussia.
23 August Germany invades France; British troops first involved in fighting – Battle of Mons.
26–29 August Russians defeated at Tannenberg.
5–10 September German advance in west halted at Battle of Marne.
9–14 September Russians defeated at Masurian Lakes.
October Trench warfare begins on the Western Front.
30 October (to 24 November) First Battle of Ypres.
20 December (to 10 March 1915) First Battle of Champagne.

1915   *23 January* Dual Alliance offensive against Russia in the Carpathians.
19 February British Navy moves into Dardanelles.
22 April (to 25 May) Second Battle of Ypres.
25 April Allied landings at Gallipoli.
22 May Russian retreat on Eastern Front begins.
23 May Italy enters war against Austria-Hungary.
23 June Italy launches first of many offensives along Isonzo River.
25 September Allied offensives begin at Loos and Champagne.
3 October Allied troops arrive at Salonika.
23 November Gallipoli evacuation begins.
27 November Collapse of Serbia.
3 December Joffre becomes French Commander-in-Chief.
17 December Haig becomes British Commander-in-Chief.

1916   *27 January* Britain introduces conscription.
21 February (to 18 December) Battle of Verdun.
4 June Russians begin Brusilov offensive.
24 June British barrage begins on the Somme.
1 July (to 13 November) Battle of the Somme.
29 August Hindenburg becomes German Commander-in-Chief.
15 September British tanks in operation for the first time (on the Somme).
3 December Nivelle becomes French Commander-in-Chief.
7 December Lloyd George replaces Asquith as British prime minister.

1917   *23 February* Germans begin withdrawal to Hindenburg Line.
12 March First Russian Revolution.
6 April USA declares war on Germany.
9 April British begin offensive at Arras.
16 April French begin offensive on the Aisne.
29 April (to 20 May) Mutinies in French armies.
15 May Pétain becomes French Commander-in-Chief.

Date	Events

8 June British capture Messines Ridge.

25 June First American troops arrive in France.

31 July (to 10 November) Third Battle of Ypres (known as Passchendaele).

24 October Italian line broken at Caporetto.

7 November Bolshevik Revolution in St Petersburg.

20 November First major tank success, at Battle of Cambrai.

2 December Fighting on Eastern Front concluded.

1918   *3 March* Russians and Germans sign Treaty of Brest-Litovsk.

21 March Germans launch Ludendorff offensive.

29 March Foch becomes Supreme Allied Commander-in-Chief on Western Front.

15 July Second Battle of the Marne begins; Germans start to retreat.

8 August Massive Allied offensive, described by Ludendorff as the 'black day of the German Army'.

26 September Final Allied offensive in the west begins.

5 October Hindenburg Line breached.

29 October (to 4 November) Battle of Vittorio Veneto – Italian advance.

30 October Turkey signs an armistice.

3 November Austria-Hungary signs an armistice.

11 November 11am Armistice begins on the Western Front.

1919   *28 June* Treaty of Versailles signed.

Glossary

Appeasement	A policy of negotiation and compromise rather than confrontation.
Armistice	A cease-fire.
Artillery	Heavy shell-firing guns which cannot be carried by soldiers.
Atrocity	An act of barbarity.
Attrition	Weakening by continual assault.
Balkans	The territory on the peninsula between the Black Sea and the Adriatic Sea.
Barrage	A wave of artillery fire from many guns.
Battalion	A unit of about 850 men.
Bayonet	A knife fixed to the end of a rifle.
Blighty	A slang British term for Britain or home (adopted from the Hindustani).
British Expeditionary Force	A small army of 150,000 men, prepared before the war broke out. It was ready to move into Europe at short notice.
Bunker	A reinforced underground shelter.
Censor	To cut out unwanted material.
Central Powers	Germany and its allies in the First World War.
Coalition	A government whose members are from more than one party.
Colony	Overseas territory administered by another country.
Conscription	Compulsory military service.
Dardanelles	The southern end of the sea passage from the Black Sea to the Mediterranean Sea.
Duckboards	Slatted wooden flooring.
Dysentery	An infection of the intestine which results in severe diarrhoea.
Entente	An agreement between nations, less formal than an alliance.
Field Marshal	The highest rank in the British Army.
Flank	The side of a military or naval formation.
Flare	A bright light fired from a gun.
Fraternization	Close association with the enemy.
Gangrene	The rotting of flesh due to loss of blood supply.
Gas gangrene	A condition in which raw flesh exposed to infection begins to rot. The only remedy before 1918 was to cut out the affected part of the body.
Grenade	A small bomb, thrown by hand.
Infantry	Soldiers who fight on foot.
Kaiser	The German emperor.
Mess tin	A metal dish in which a soldier cooked and ate his food.
Mobilize	To make armed forces ready for war.
Morale	State of mental preparedness and confidence.
Mortar	A short-range muzzle-loading cannon. Shells fired from it have a high flight path.
No man's land	The land between two opposing lines of trenches.
Offensive	A major attack.
Ottoman Empire	The former Turkish empire which included modern Turkey and parts of south-eastern Europe, Asia and Africa. It existed from the late thirteenth century until the end of the First World War.

Pacifism	Not believing in war or the use of force.
Parapet	The low wall at the front of a trench.
Platoon	A unit of 30–40 men.
Propaganda	Information slanted to favour one point of view.
Round	A bullet or artillery shell.
Scapegoat	Someone or something made to bear the blame for others' mistakes.
Schlieffen Plan	The German plan, drawn up before the outbreak of war in 1914, to defeat France quickly by attacking from the north-west through Belgium.
Self determination	The right of a nation to choose its own form of government, without interference from foreign powers.
Shell	A large missile fired from a gun, which explodes on impact.
Shrapnel	Fragments of an exploding shell or bomb.
Sniper	A solitary marksman.
Stalemate	A situation where no side is able to gain an advantage.
Strategy	Overall military plan.

Further reading

Easier Works
Bates, B., *The First World War*, Blackwell, 1984
Evans, D., *The Great War 1914–18*, Edward Arnold, 1981
Gibson, M., *The First World War*, Wayland, 1985
Mair, C., *Britain at War*, Murray, 1982
Martin, C., *Battle of the Somme*, Wayland, 1983
Ross, S.(ed.), *The First World War*, Wayland, 1989

Other General Secondary Sources
Bourne, J.M., *Britain and the Great War*, EdwardArnold, 1989
Bruce, A., *An Illustrated Companion to the First World War*, Michael Joseph, 1989
Ellis, J., *Eye-deep in Hell: Life in the Trenches 1914–1918*, Fontana, 1977
Fussell, P., *The Great War and Modern Memory*, OUP, 1975
Gilbert, M., *First World War Atlas*, Weidenfeld and Nicholson, 1970
Keegan, J., *The Face of Battle*, Cape, 1976
Liddell Hart, H.B., *History of the World War 1914–1918*, Faber, 1934
Lloyd, A., *The War in the Trenches*, Granada, 1976
Taylor, A.J.P., *The First World War*, Penguin, 1966
Winter, D., *Death's Men, Soldiers of the Great War*, Allen Lane, 1979

Works on Specific Topics
Ashworth, A., *The Sociology of Trench Warfare*, Macmillan, 1980
Ellis, J., *The Social History of the Machine Gun*, Croom Helm, 1975
Fitzsimons, B. (ed), *Tanks and Weapons of World War One*, Phoebus, 1975
Leed, E.J., *No Man's Land*, CUP, 1979
Liddle, P.H., *The Soldier's War, 1914–18*, Blandford Press, 1988
Macdonald, L., *Somme*, Michael Joseph, 1983
Simkins, P., *Kitchener's Army*, Manchester University Press, 1989
Winter, J., *Lloyd George and the Generals*, Associated University Press, 1983
Terraine, J., *Douglas Haig. The Educated Soldier*, Hutchinson, 1963

Original Sources
Chapman, G. (ed), *Vain Glory*, Cassell, 1937
Graves, R., *Goodbye To All That*, Penguin, 1960
Hibberd, D. and Onions, J. (eds), *Poetry of the Great War: An Anthology*, Macmillan, 1986
Lloyd George, D., *War Memoirs*, 2 vols., Odhams, 1938
Ludendorff, E., *My War Memories*, 2 vols., Hutchinson, n.d..
Macdonald, L. (ed.), *1914–1918 Voices and Images of the Great War*, Michael Joseph, 1988
Remarque, E.M., *All Quiet on the Western Front*, Putnam, 1929
Sassoon, S., *Memoirs of an Infantry Officer*, Faber, 1930
Sherriff, R.C., *Journey's End*, 1929
Williamson, H., *The Wet Flanders Plain*, Faber, 1929

Notes on sources

1 Brown, M. and Seaton, S., *The Christmas Truce*, Secker and Warburg, 1984, p.10.
2 Graves, Robert, *Goodbye To All That,* Penguin, 1960, p.85.
3 Bourne, J.M., *Britain and the Great War 1914–1918*, Edward Arnold, 1989, p.165.
4 Macdonald, Lyn, *1914–1918 Voices and Images of the Great War*, Michael Joseph, 1988, p.255.
5 Bourne, op.cit., pp.166, 168.
6 Macdonald, op.cit., p.244.
7 Bourne, op.cit., p.166.
8 Ellis, J., *The Social History of the Machine Gun*, Croom Helm, 1975, p.123.
9 *Ibid.*, p.136.
10 *Ibid.*, p.111.
11 Song quoted in *Oh What A Lovely War*, Eyre Methuen, 1967.
12 Sassoon, Siegfried *Memoirs of an Infantry Officer*, Faber, 1965, pp 49–50.
13 Lloyd, A., *War in the Trenches*, Granada, 1976, p.51.
14 Bourne, op. cit., pp 158–9.
15 Chapman, G., (ed.), *Vain Glory*, Cassell, 1937, pp.464–5.
16 Lloyd, op. cit., p.163.
17 Terraine, J., *The Smoke and the Fire. Myths and Anti-Myths of War 1861–1945*, Sidgwick and Jackson, 1980, p.108.
18 Taylor, A.J.P., *The First World War*, Penguin, 1966 p.140.
19 Ellis, op. cit. p.67.
20 Macdonald, op.cit., p.81.
21 *Ibid.*, p.104.
22 *Ibid.*, p.222.
23 All excerpts from ibid., p.168.
24 Bruce, A., *An Illustrated Companion To The First World War*, Michael Joseph, 1989, p.374.
25 Taylor, op. cit., p.68.
26 Graves, op. cit., pp. 83–4.
27 *Ibid.*, p.96.
28 Lloyd, op.cit., p.31.
29 Macdonald, op.cit., p.100.
30 Bourne, op. cit., p.223.
31 Lloyd, op. cit., pp. 125, 127.
32 *Ibid.*, p.123.
33 From 'Exposure'.
34 Second Lieutenant A.S.C. Fox quoted in Liddle, P.H., *The Soldier's War, 1914–18*, Blandford Press, 1988, p.68.
35 Brown and Seaton, op. cit., pp 71–2.
36 *Ibid.*, p.194.
37 Graves, op. cit. p.131.
38 Bruce, op. cit., p.86.
39 Graves, op. cit., p.95.
40 *Ibid.*, p.95.
41 Taylor, op. cit., p.140.
42 Quoted in *Oh What A Lovely War*.
43 Bourne, op. cit., p.223.
44 *Ibid.*, p.214.
45 Macdonald, op. cit., p.53.
46 Sassoon, op. cit., pp 177–8.
47 Bourne, op. cit., p.173.
48 Lloyd George, D., *War Memoirs*, Odhams, 1938, Vol. 1, p.536.
49 Taylor, op. cit., p.163.
50 *Ibid.*, pp.218–9.
51 *Ibid.*, p.219.
52 From 'The Soldier'.

Index

Figures in **bold** refer to illustrations.

Acknowledgements

The author and publisher gratefully acknowledge the following for permission to reprint copyright material: Faber & Faber Ltd and K.S. Giniger Co Inc for extracts from Siegfried Sassoon's *Memoirs of an Infantry Officer* and A.P. Watt Ltd, on behalf of the Trustees of the Robert Graves Copyright Trust for extracts from Robert Graves' *Goodbye To All That*. The author and publisher would also like to thank the following for allowing their illustrations to be reproduced in this book: Bridgeman Art Library 38; Camera Press 23 (top), 27, 36, 37 (top), 45 (top), 47; Mary Evans 7, 18, 29, 39, 51; Hulton-Deutsch 15 (top), 21, 41, 43 (top), 50, 54, 55; Imperial War Museum 12, 13, 15 (bottom), 16, 19, 22, 23 (bottom), 24, 25, 28, 30, 31, 32, 33, 34, 35, 42; Peter Newark's Military Archive *cover*, 14, 48, 49; Popperfoto 17, 53; Punch 40, 43 (bottom), 45 (bottom), 46; Weimar Archive 5 (bottom), 8, 9, 11, 20, 37 (bottom). The maps were drawn by Peter Bull.